What Does It Mean to Be Present?

by Rana DiOrio   Illustrated by Eliza Wheeler

Little Pickle Press

What does it mean to be present?

oes it mean showing up in class? No.

Does it mean sharing something at show-and-tell? No.

Does it mean wrapping yourself up? **NO!**

Being present means...

...listening carefully when other people are speaking.

...noticing when someone needs help and
taking the time to give them the help they need.

...focusing on what's happening now,
    instead of thinking about what's next.

...appreciating what you have,
even if what someone else
has seems better.

...waiting patiently for your turn.

...treating each new experience as an opportunity,

and understanding that making mistakes is how we learn and grow.

...being grateful for your
family and friends
and telling them so.

...savoring each bite of your delicious food.

...cuddling with your puppy and enjoying
how soft and wriggly he feels.

...relishing the warmth of the sun and the sound of the rain.

...feeling the sand between your toes,
    watching the rolling waves,
        smelling the briny seaweed,

listening to the cawing seagulls,
    and tasting the ocean's salty spray.

...allowing the rhythm of your breath...
in and out, in and out...
to make you feel peaceful.

...closing your eyes and being
    still enough to hear your inner voice.

Being present means living in the moment.
It means realizing that

yesterday is history,
tomorrow is a mystery,

and today is a gift—that's why we call it the present!

So tell your friends what it means to be present.

And spread the word!

When we're all present, life can be
much richer, fuller, and happier!

Being Present

Did you notice the blue butterfly that reappears throughout *What Does It Mean to Be Present?* What does this butterfly make you think of? The simple act of noticing what is occurring in our environment is an easy way to become more present in our daily lives. How does the world around us change as one season passes to the next? What symbols do you see displayed during various holidays? Children and adults may not always see these small changes. Listening, noticing, and being aware of what is happening in the moment are ways that all of us can try to be more present every day. By focusing on and enjoying the present, we can make more meaningful use of our time.

What You Can Do

Being present in your life can take some practice. Here are some simple ways you can practice being present.

1. **Focus.** Communication is an important part of being present. What makes someone a good listener? Why is it important to listen to others? What happens when multiple people start talking at once? Practice talking with a friend, family member, or teacher. Listen to what the person has to say. Can you repeat exactly what they've said? Try communicating with someone when there is loud noise in the room like a television or tablet. Is it harder or easier to concentrate? Our body language also says a lot about whether we're paying attention. What can you do with your body to show that you're present? What does a person's body look like when they're not listening? What are ways people show they're listening in other cultures?

2. **Awareness.** Noticing the world around you and how it changes is another important part of being present. It's how we "live in the moment." One exercise you can try to help you better understand the passing of time is timing your stillness. Ask a friend or caring adult to help you by being a time keeper. They will need a clock or stopwatch. Decide on a number of minutes you'd like to be still—two or three minutes is a great way to start for this activity. When you close your eyes, your time keeper starts timing your stillness. Open your eyes when you think your time is done. How much time had passed? What made you think your time had passed? What were you concentrating on during that time? Did the actual two or three minutes seem long or short to you? You can also practice awareness by keeping a journal for one week to track how much time you spend eating, sleeping, playing, bathing, learning, etc., each day. You might be surprised by how much time you use for each activity. What else might you do with your time?

3. **Use your senses.** We think of the five senses as sight, smell, sound, taste, and touch. Each of these senses help us experience the world around us and helps us to be mindful of our environment. How do you use your senses each day? Do you remember any interesting sights or sounds you heard today? Try sitting still and think about what you are experiencing with each of your senses. What do you see? Hear? Smell? Feel? Taste? Try walking outside and asking yourself the same questions. What do you notice when you are conscious of using your five senses? Practice using your senses each day to experience the world in new ways.

These are just a few ways you can practice being present. But these aren't the only ways! There are lots of things you can do to slow down and live fully in every moment. Always be on the lookout for new ways to enjoy our daily experiences and make the world an even happier place!

For more information, including lesson plans, please visit LittlePicklePress.com.

About the Author

Rana DiOrio is skilled in the art of multitasking. In 1999, while sitting by the pool during a much-needed weekend away with a close friend, she was pecking away at her phone when her friend turned to her and asked, "Does that device float?" Rana stopped working and started to enjoy the moment. "It's so easy to get swept up in the swift pace of life," Rana explains. "I hope *What Does It Mean to Be Present?* conveys the importance of slowing down, being mindful, and savoring every moment."

Rana has written her way through life—as a student, lawyer, banker, investor, and now as an author and entrepreneur. She enjoys fitness training, yoga, and reading nonfiction and children's books. Rana is passionate about dreaming big dreams and helping other entrepreneurs realize their own dreams. She lives in San Francisco, California, with her three children. Follow her on Twitter @ranadiorio.

About the Illustrator

Eliza Wheeler was raised in the north woods of Wisconsin in a family of musicians, artists, and teachers. Drawing was her favorite form of play as a child, her emotional outlet as a teen, and is her passion as an adult. Some of her strongest creative influences have been the wild Wisconsin seasons, canoeing the Brule River, picking blueberries with her grandmother, and digging through the snow with her brothers. Eliza received her BFA in Graphic Design at the University of Wisconsin-Stout in 2006, and began to pursue a career in illustration in 2009, when she found her true calling—illustrating children's books. She has written and illustrated the *New York Times* bestseller, *Miss Maple's Seeds*, and has illustrated many other picture books and novels, including Alison McGhee's *Tell Me A Tattoo Story*, Pat Zietlow Miller's *Wherever You Go*, and Holly Black's Newbery Honor–winning *Doll Bones*.

Eliza finds that she is most present when meditating, in nature, on walks, reading books, being cozy, and with her husband, Adam. They enjoy spending their time between the riverbanks of Wisconsin, and the coasts of California.

Discover more of the award-winning
What Does It Mean to Be...? series

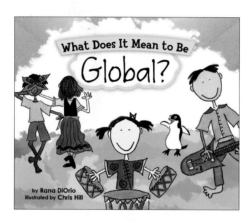

What Does It Mean to Be
Global?
by Rana DiOrio
Illustrated by Chris Hill

What Does It Mean to Be
Green?
by Rana DiOrio
Illustrated by Chris Blair

What Does It Mean to Be an
Entrepreneur?
"Inspires young dreamers to find
the courage to be doers."
–Jerry Greenfield,
Co-Founder, Ben & Jerry's
by Rana DiOrio & Emma D. Dryden • Illustrated by Ken Min

What Does It Mean to Be
Kind?
"A beautiful book with
a beautiful message."
–R. J. Palacio
#1 New York Times
bestselling author of
Wonder
by Rana DiOrio • Illustrated by Stéphane Jorisch

For Kara, whose talent, charisma, mettle, and presence inspire me.
— R.D.

For my family, who has believed in my abilities since day one.
— E.W.

Copyright © 2010, 2020 by March 4th, Inc.
Cover and internal design © 2017, 2020 by Sourcebooks
Text by Rana DiOrio
Illustrated by Eliza Wheeler

Sourcebooks, Little Pickle Press, and the colophon are registered trademarks of Sourcebooks

Published by Little Pickle Press, an imprint of Sourcebooks Kids
P.O. Box 4410, Naperville, Illinois 60567-4410
(630) 961-3900
sourcebookskids.com

Library of Congress Cataloging-in-Publication Data is on file with the publisher.

Source of Production: Shenzhen Wing King Tong Paper Products Co. Ltd.,
Shenzhen, Guangdong Province, China
Date of Production: December 2019
Run Number: 5017164

Printed and bound in China.
WKT 10 9 8 7 6 5 4 3 2 1